Heather Emge

Performing between the Acts

Heather Emge

Performing between the Acts

Issues of Personal Identity
and Performance in Frances Burney's
The Wanderer, or Female Difficulties (1814)

VDM Verlag Dr. Müller

Imprint

Bibliographic information by the German National Library: The German National Library lists this publication at the German National Bibliography; detailed bibliographic information is available on the Internet at http://dnb.d-nb.de.
 Any brand names and product names mentioned in this book are subject to trademark, brand or patent protection and are trademarks or registered trademarks of their respective holders. The use of brand names, product names, common names, trade names, product descriptions etc. even without a particular marking in this works is in no way to be construed to mean that such names may be regarded as unrestricted in respect of trademark and brand protection legislation and could thus be used by anyone.

Cover image: www.purestockx.com

Publisher:
VDM Verlag Dr. Müller Aktiengesellschaft & Co. KG
Dudweiler Landstr. 125 a, 66123 Saarbrücken, Germany
Phone +49 681 9100-698, Fax +49 681 9100-988, Email: info@vdm-verlag.de

Copyright © 2008 VDM Verlag Dr. Müller Aktiengesellschaft & Co. KG and licensors
All rights reserved. Saarbrücken 2008

Produced in USA and UK by:
Lightning Source Inc., La Vergne, Tennessee, USA
Lightning Source UK Ltd., Milton Keynes, UK

ISBN: 978-3-8364-6764-3

Abstract

In her final novel The Wanderer, or Female Difficulties (1814), Frances Burney addresses contemporary philosophies of personal identity in complex ways that expose the ambiguities inherent in eighteenth-century notions of the self. Burney engages, tests, and challenges the concepts of the self-in-consciousness and the abject self to expose problems and complexities within contemporary discourses. Issues of performance, performativity, and theatricality are also explored within the narrative to expose complexities concerning the role of agency in the creation, profession, and perpetuation of personal identity. Several ways in which Burney experiments with narrative form and the relationship between the text and the reader are also investigated, especially techniques related to the construction and employment of the narrator.

Acknowledgments

This thesis could not have been written without
the tireless enthusiasm, assistance, and support of Dr. Richard Eversole,
who has helped me to see literature in new ways and whose wealth of knowledge has
proven invaluable to my understanding of the historical, theoretical, and literary
contexts of Frances Burney's complex works.
I have enduring gratitude for the time, guidance, and encouragement
that Dr. Eversole has provided me during this long and rewarding project.

The support of committee members
Dr. Dorice W. Elliott and Dr. Richard F. Hardin,
along with their encouragement and insightful commentary,
has also proven invaluable to the completion and improvement of this work,
as well as to the success of my other academic efforts.
I am grateful for their time and consideration.

I am also grateful to my many mentors, friends, and colleagues
at The University of Kansas who have provided me with support and inspiration
throughout my academic career,
including Dr. Marjorie Swann, who has given me
sincere encouragement, criticism, and guidance that has helped me to become
a stronger student, scholar, teacher, and person.

I also extend thanks to my friends and family members
for their understanding, support and encouragement,
and especially to Mark Emge, who always cheers me on
in everything that I attempt to do.

"...one is always and everywhere, more or less consciously, playing a role...It is in these roles that we know each other; it is in these roles that we know ourselves. Our very faces are living masks, which...tend more and more to conform to the type we are seeking to impersonate...In a sense, and in so far as this mask represents the conception we have formed of ourselves—the role we are striving to live up to—this mask is our truer self, the self we would like to be. In the end, our conception of our role becomes second nature to our personality."—Robert Park

"There has been very great Reason, on several Accounts, for the learned World to endeavour at settling what it was that might be said to compose personal Identity."
—Anonymous, Spectator, No. 578

Throughout her literary career, Frances Burney (1752-1840) wrote numerous plays and letters, in addition to four novels. Her first novel, Evelina, written in epistolary form and published anonymously in 1778, is inarguably her most widely read work in present day classrooms and scholarship. Despite its popularity, however, Burney's subsequent novels, Cecilia, or the Memoirs of an Heiress (1782), Camilla, or A Picture of Youth (1796), and her most experimental in terms of content and scope, The Wanderer, or Female Difficulties (1814), each of which depart from the epistolary form into third person narrative, are relatively only rarely considered,. All four of these novels have been identified throughout scholarship as Bildugsroman and, more particularly, narrative explorations of the particular challenges faced by women in eighteenth-century Britain. Indeed, all depict young woman protagonists throughout their respective coming-of-age journeys that are each continually fraught with crises and struggles, all moving toward and ending with establishment in an economically-secure and socially-desirable marriage arrangement and an implied subsequent launch into bourgeois domestic prosperity and bliss. Also emphasized in all of these novels are the multifarious challenges and obstacles that are encountered by the heroines in their quest to navigate what is depicted as the often brutal and suffocating patriarchal social structures that, for these women, inhibit everything from financial and legal independence to personal expression.

While obviously valid and helpful in understanding these novels as deft commentaries on particular social and political circumstances of eighteenth-century British society, such interpretations, when taken as definitive, can also threaten to reduce the philosophical complexities and subtle nuances of Burney's work. In fact, these texts, especially The Wanderer, also seem to exist as agents through which complex philosophical issues are raised, tested, and challenged, especially those surrounding the nature of personal identity, creating an intriguing dialogue between various philosophies of the self that permeated intellectual thought and speculation of the period. Inextricably linked to these issues of identity and self are issues of performance, performativity, and theatricality, all concerns in which Burney was well-versed, being a prolific author of many dramatic pieces, as well as an occasional actress and frequent audience member of popular theatrical entertainments. When viewed in this way, the depth and complexity of these narratives is substantially expanded. Careful analysis of the ways in which these issues are treated in these texts proves to become quite complicated rather quickly. It seems that Burney, rather than making any definitive argument or statement in acceptance or dismissal of any particular philosophical tenet, instead succeeds in exposing ambiguities and conflicts that arise when any one idea is applied in a practical manner. In doing so, Burney figuratively highlights important nuances related to issues of performance and performativity and their roles in the creation, profession, and perpetuation of personal identity, as well as exposes complexities in the related contemporary philosophical notions of the self.

 This ambiguity is created by the narrative presentation of a series of problems and demonstrations of different philosophical views that can be validly interpreted in multiple ways. This oftentimes creates the condition that one interpretation of a specific scene or narrative circumstance can be viewed as equally plausible as its converse, thus leaving the reader without a clear understanding of a definitive implicit statement, but with a questioning instead. Because of this inherent quality in the novel, I do not intend to present a linear argument that would, inevitably, compress and condense the complexities of the various narrative circumstances and the accompanying implicit philosophical commentary, distorting important nuances in the process. Instead, I intend to offer some considerations and reconsiderations of a number of the ways in which issues of identity construction, profession, and perpetuation, along with the accompanying issues of performance, performativity, and theatricality, are presented throughout <u>The Wanderer</u> in order to bring out and articulate the philosophical and theoretical ambiguities that are inherent in Burney's complex narrative.

 Throughout <u>The Wanderer</u>, as well as in Burney's earlier novels, performance, both social and theatrical, is constantly foregrounded, clearly indicating its thematic importance. Overt theatrical and musical performances figure prominently in the plot of <u>The Wanderer</u>, including the drawing room performance of Colley Cibber's play <u>The Provoked Husband</u> (1728) that is instigated by Elinor

Joddrell and performed by many of the main characters, Juliet's scheduled concert performance (as Ellis), and the many other formal operas, concerts, and plays of which Juliet and the other characters comprise the attendant audiences. In addition to these clearly delineated instances of organized theatrical and musical performance, social performances, whether the products of deliberately construed and executed patterns of behavior or more unconscious adherences to social conventions, are also highlighted, though perhaps less explicitly. Critical exploration of the various performances, then, is necessary to approach a more complete understanding of the nuances of the already sensational plot of The Wanderer, which, fittingly, features a heroine whose name, and, perhaps, identity shift all the way through the long narrative. Through careful consideration of the various instances in the narrative that involve some sort of performance, whether theatrical or social in nature, much can be learned about the complexities, ambiguities and paradoxes of identity that Burney seems to raise throughout all of her novels, but perhaps most complexly in The Wanderer, her last.

Most readers of The Wanderer have identified one significant narrative focus to be the protagonist's ever-shifting name and what may seem to some as her equally amorphous identity.[1] In her influential critical work on Burney's novels The Iron Pen: Frances Burney and The Politics of Women's Writing, Julia Epstein explains that "Naming is never a simple process in [Burney's] novels, tied as it is to the empowering social institutions of class, family, marriage, lineage, and inheritance,"

---

[1] For the sake of preserving organizational and narrative continuity, I will refer to the protagonist as "Juliet" throughout this paper.

and noting that "Juliet has no full name for most of <u>The Wanderer</u>…not until the final volume does anyone address her by her proper name" (3, 178). Entering the narrative as a disembodied voice, Juliet is known only as "The Wanderer" or "The Incognita" through much of the beginning chapters. She then becomes known as "Ellis" through a complicated process that I shall deal with in detail later on, and even during the comparatively lengthy period that she is known to others by this appellative, it undergoes subtle yet significant variations. Following this period, Juliet becomes known, in different instances, by no less than four other proper names, including, finally, her birth name of Juliet Granville. Because proper names are considered as closely tied to personal identity in modern Western societies, the problem of Juliet's behavior as it relates to her identity or various identities is implicitly presented to both the reader and to the characters with whom she comes into contact. This general problem has many interrelated facets. One essential aspect of this problem can perhaps be stated most clearly in the form of a question: Does Juliet deliberately construct and perform various identities throughout the narrative and, if so, for what purpose(s)? In other words, does Juliet consciously act out various characters, passing them off as her true self, with the intent to deceive other characters into believing that she is a different person from who she knows herself to be? Or is she only viewed as attempting to deceive others in such a way, actually only acting ingenuously as herself throughout?

    Several scholars have argued that Juliet does intentionally construct various identities for herself, including one named "Ellis," and subsequently perform them consciously throughout the narrative with the intent to deliberately deceive others in order to promote various forms of personal gain. Kathleen Anderson, for one, in her article "Frances Burney's The Wanderer: Actress as Virtuous Deceiver," goes so far as to state that "[The Wanderer] is a novel about a woman whose precarious and even tragic wanderings evoke her creative powers of self-representation" and that "[Juliet's] ability to perform a range of parts with quickness and credibility saves her life and the lives of other central characters" (424). Another scholar, Mascha Gemmeke, operating along a similar interpretative line, declares that "Juliet's metamorphoses also reveal her personal struggle to establish a social identity," implying, then, that these transformations are deliberately and knowingly instigated by Juliet (213).

    These interpretations are accurate for several specific instances in the novel in which Juliet does consciously create alter-identities for herself and clearly performs them with premeditated effort. Interestingly, two of the most obvious instances involve Juliet's creation and adoption of elaborate costumes; the act of doing so, as one scholar has argued, can be viewed as "the most explicit external sign of her embrasure of performance" (Anderson 437). One of the most apparent instances of this type of acting becomes apparent soon after the opening scene in which Juliet appears as a nameless "Incognita," boarding the boat of refugees after having tinted her skin to appear as if she is of African or West Indian descent, covered her countenance with bandages, and donned "the most ordinary" clothing that largely obscures her claim to her true higher social class (Burney 12). Her attire significantly disguises her face, as described by the narrator, who states that she wears "…a French night-cap, which had almost concealed all her features," along with "a large black patch, that covered half her left cheek, and a broad black ribbon, which bound a bandage of cloth over the right side of her forehead," while her body paint, perhaps the most extreme trapping of her disguise, is described as tinting her skin "so dark a colour, that [it] might rather be styled black than brown" (19-20). The nature of her appearance is quickly noted by the other characters who occupy the boat; they almost immediately begin speculation about her social class, her nationality, and even her religious orientation, as Elinor, seeing that Juliet in the attitude of prayer, declares that "'she's a nun, then, depend upon it,'" while Harleigh believes her to be an escaped prisoner and some of the others believe her to be "an adventurer" and "a foreigner" with all negative connotations of those terms intended by them (13, 20, 26, 33). At this point in the narrative, neither the characters nor the reader are definitively aware that Juliet is in disguise, as her appearance is simply described, with no indication from the narrator that she should be suspected of disguise. Later, however, her particular appearance is proven to both the characters and the reader to be an elaborate disguise, as the body paint wears off, revealing "skin changed from a tint nearly black, to the brightest, whitest, and most dazzling fairness" and, soon after, the bandages accidentally fall off, exposing "neither wound, scar, nor injury of any sort" (43-44). The emphasis placed on these details of Juliet's disguise betray the elaborate planning and execution that would have gone into adorning herself in such a manner, thus undoubtedly showing her to have, in this instance, performed with an intent to deceive those around her in regard to her true identity.

Other sets of related instances in which Juliet deliberately and consciously creates and performs identities other than her own with the intent to deceive those who encounter her occur much later in the novel, after she has been known to both the inhabitants of Brighthelmstone and to the reader as "Ellis." After living and working in various capacities amongst the group of central characters in Brighthelmstone, Juliet leaves for London in search of new employment and escape from an increasingly undesirable and intolerable social situation, having been ostracized from popular society due to negative speculation about her background. Providentially, she locates her childhood friend Gabriella, who has established a haberdasher's shop, of which Juliet happily becomes partner after a decidedly joyful reunion with one who knows her true identity. Her elation is cut short, however, when advertisements appear in the newspapers and on flyers posted around London that call for her arrest, declaring her to be a fugitive from her husband. Not safe around anyone who might recognize her as the woman described on the flyers, Juliet, horror-stricken and "making up a packet of linen to carry in her hand, and hanging a loaded work-bag upon her arm," decides that she "'must fly;—instantly fly!'" (654). Before assuming a disguise aimed at thwarting detection, the narrator emphasizes Juliet's essential transformation, stating that she "became again a Wanderer," as she makes her way to Salisbury with the intent to "lodge herself in the first clean cottage which could afford her a room," and subsequently moves on into the New Forest in search of further obscurity (654-655). She soon finds that she must continue her journey, however, after the woman with whom she lodges for three days recognizes her as "a person advertised in the London news-papers" (662). At this moment, Juliet "resolve[s], with whatever fatigue, to travel on foot, that she might not hazard being recognized, through the advertisement" and dons a deliberate disguise with the aim of deceiving those with whom she might come into contact (665). This action is carefully framed as conscious, planned, and deliberate by the narrator, who states "to be less liable to detection from passing observers, she changed, over night, her bonnet, which was of white chip, for one the most coarse and ordinary of straw, with her young hostess; of whom, also, she bought a blue striped apron" (665). She continues on in this guise for awhile, until she later "[gives] a commission, to the younger mistress of the house [in which she briefly lodges], to purchase her some ready-made linen," out of which she fashions a "homely" dress in which she is described as "more consistently equipped" as one belonging to the lower class of the people among whom she travels (672). Her disguise is soon shown to be successful in separate instances where denizens of the New Forest mistake her for Deb Dyson, a young woman of ill-repute who lives in the New Forest (677). Her physical dress is only part of her disguise, however; Juliet also modifies her behavior slightly with the intent of appearing to be more like the rustic people with whom she finds herself, clearly using her powers of perception and analysis in multiple instances to shift her appearance and behavior according to her immediate surroundings and to thus perform particular identities to control the behavior of others in relation to herself. In these instances, then, Juliet is clearly shown to again consciously manipulate both her appearance and behavior in order to appear as one clearly distinct from her true demeanor and social class. This dissonance is heightened by the condition that the reader has previously been made aware of Juliet's true identity during the semi-climactic scene in which Juliet confirms Gabriella's revelation to the sympathetic and interested Sir Jasper Harrington that she is, in truth, the legitimate daughter of "the Earl of Melbury's only son, Lord Granville" (641). Thus, the reader is acutely aware that for Juliet to adopt the dress and demeanor of a rustic forest-dweller is, undoubtedly, an instance of drastic performance, one that is clearly driven with the interests of perpetuating deception to achieve self-preservation.

Despite these instances in which it is clear that Juliet consciously conceives and performs alternate identities with the intention of deceiving others for personal gain, it seems inaccurate to claim, as several scholars do[2], that she similarly creates and performs all of the various identities by which she is known and understood by the characters with which she comes into contact throughout the narrative and by the reader of the novel. In some circumstances, whether Juliet consciously intends to perform as another character in order to deceive others into believing that she is someone who she is not is decidedly ambiguous. The most telling circumstance in which Juliet does not seem to consciously perform as an alter-identity is the long

---

[2] Notable among these critics are Mascha Gemmeke, who, in Frances Burney and the Female Bildugsroman: An Interpretation of *The Wanderer, or Female Difficulties*, states that Juliet "masquerad[es] as Ellis," and Kathleen Anderson, who argues that "Juliet accepts [the] mistake [that others have made in calling her 'Ellis'] willingly, because it prevents her from committing the 'deceit' of designating a name for herself" (Gemmeke 221; Anderson 439).

period during which she is known as "Ellis," a character whose foundational trait is that of belonging to a slightly lower class than that of the particular elite social set with whom Juliet interacts while in Brighthelmstone. Instead of deliberately conceiving of an alternate identity, naming it "Ellis" and subsequently performing as that preconceived character in order to deceive others, Juliet seems to adopt a different stance in relation to that identity. In contrast to the nameless fugitive identity in which she enters the novel and the various New Forest identities that she adopts later, the Ellis identity seems largely unperformed, or at least not performed consciously, by Juliet, who also never seems to overtly assume any characteristics related to an alternate identity during this period. Instead, the Ellis identity seems to be created, professed, and perpetuated for her than overtly created, defined, and maintained by her.

  That the Ellis identity is created and established for Juliet is most clear when one considers the very birth of the name "Ellis" as used in the context of Juliet's story. The mischievous young rake Ireton originates the name during the intensely fraught period when Juliet and the other characters aboard the refugee boat arrive in Brighthelmstone. During the ocean voyage and the days following the refugees' arrival in England, all of the characters with whom Juliet comes into contact are extremely preoccupied with discovering her name, background, and identity. Instigating the action that leads to the creation of the Ellis name is the constantly prying Miss Bydel, who demands of Juliet that she declare her name, stating to her "'your name, at least, can be no such great secret, for you must be called something or other'" (81). Ireton promptly interjects, declaring "'I will tell you what her name is, Miss Bydel; 'tis L.S.,'" thus taking the initials that he saw in the address of a letter that Juliet accepts unequivocally as its intended recipient (81). The transformation of these two initials into the name "Ellis" is purely accidental, the result of a mistaken interpretation, as pointed out by the narrator, who states, "Miss Bydel, not comprehending that Ireton meant two initial letters, said, 'Elless? Well I see no reason why any body should be ashamed to own their name is Elless'" (81). The error is noted by both Ireton and Selina Joddrell, the youngest inhabitant of the house in which Juliet finds shelter, but they both make a conscious decision to allow the mistake to pass, as the narrator notes that "Selina, tittering, would have cleared up the mistake; but Ireton, laughing yet more heartily, made her a sign to let it pass" (81). This early form of the name, "Elless," is transformed imperceptibly by a similar type of aural mistake into "Ellis," after a brief span during which Juliet is again referred to as "the stranger," and the name adheres, first overtly sanctioned by Miss Arbe, who, after calling Juliet by the name of "Ellis," explains to her "'for they have all settled…that your real name is Ellis'" and soon after adopted and perpetuated by Elinor, who, the narrator explains "would only call the stranger Miss Ellis, a name which, she said, she verily believed that Miss Bydel, with all her stupidity, had hit upon, and which therefore, henceforth, should be adopted" (81-83). Clearly, then, Juliet herself had no active part in creating or promoting the name of "Ellis" as her own; instead, it is evident that it is created for and conferred upon her by those who are ignorant of her true identity and who, significantly, accept and believe that "Ellis" is truly her rightful name.

During this time in which the name of "Ellis" is created and quickly bestowed upon her, Juliet acts in a purely passive manner, remaining silent as she is called by the various derivations of "Ellis" by the several attendant characters and even "[dropping] her eyes" at Miss Bydel's first utterance of it (81). Significantly, the name is created and attached to Juliet during the scene in which she is goaded into participating in a drawing room theatrical production of Colley Cibber's The Provoked Husband (1728), first, only as prompter and musical performer for the intermissions between acts, though the leading role of Lady Townly is soon forced upon her acceptance (81-83). When the parallel actions of the scene are viewed together, they can be seen to operate as metaphorical in the sense that Juliet, while overtly assigned the theatrical roles of prompter, musical performer, and Lady Townly, she is also, in essence though less overtly, assigned the role of Ellis by the other characters. In fact, it is, fittingly, the actress and theatrical director Miss Arbe who first calls Juliet by the name of "Ellis" directly to her face and who insists that everyone who knows of her believes that "Ellis" is "[her] real name," further emphasizing that Juliet has been figuratively cast in the role of Ellis by those who surround her (82). Miss Arbe's further insistence that since Juliet "'is so clever,…she shall perform between the acts'" of the theatrical production suggests metaphorically that Juliet, since she is referred to and believed to be someone named "Ellis" by those who surround her, will similarly "perform between the acts" of her true existence as

Ellis, those metaphorical "acts" being her former life in France and the period of stability in which she finds herself at the end of the novel (81). Though Juliet overtly accepts the parts of prompter, musical performer, and Lady Townly while consciously aware of their contrived nature, she never overtly accepts the name and the accompanying social role of "Ellis"; in fact, she never refers to herself by that name or gives any indication, oral or otherwise, that she willfully appropriates it. In this sense, then, a subtle suggestion is made through these narrative circumstances that Juliet cannot truly and consciously perform an artificially-constructed role of "Ellis" in the same ways that she will perform the various theatrical roles that she has been assigned since she does not accept it as akin to those that she recognizes as overtly theatrical.

Juliet's lack of agency in creating and perpetuating the "Ellis" identity is also underscored in this scene, and in others, by her disgust with the very suggestion of overt and deliberate performance. Juliet's reluctance to perform theatrically in any capacity is emphasized repeatedly in this particular episode by the narrator, who relates that Juliet "declare[s] her utter inability to comply with such a request," though she is soon bullied into accepting the roles, albeit grudgingly, as is narrated: "she could not refuse, but her compliance was without any sort of exertion, from a desire to avoid, not promote similar calls for exhibition" (82). Her repugnance to overt performance, thus made so clear, further suggests that Juliet would be unlikely to submit herself to such an extended and continuous conscious performance of another personal identity, in this case, that of "Ellis."

Yet this interpretation of her indicative revulsion becomes fraught with contradiction when it is noted that Juliet displays the same type of abhorrence towards overt performance when she disguises herself during her escape into the New Forest. After Juliet dons the disguise by which she is later taken for the wench Deb Dyson, the narrator describes Juliet's attendant feelings, stating that "shocking to all her feelings was this attempt at disguise, so imitative of guilt, so full of semblance to conscious imposture" (665). Though she clearly feels the same type of abhorrence against deliberately assuming and performing the identity of another, Juliet in this instance, persists in her conscious disguise as a forest dweller to retain her safety. So, since she is willing to perform with the intent to deceive in this situation, why would she not be willing to consciously perform the "Ellis" identity? Perhaps the two situations require different considerations; in the New Forest flight scenes, Juliet is clearly framed as facing a period of extreme danger, both of being captured by her adversary and of encountering bodily harm from those she meets along the way. This qualifying circumstance is further emphasized later, following her retreat from the dangerous forest. Having been recognized and subsequently rescued by the benevolent Sir Jasper Harrington and the incorrigible Riley, Juliet recognizes the suddenly ineffectual state of her disguise, as the narrator glosses her reasoning by stating, "What she had been seen and discovered in, could no longer serve any purpose of concealment," further qualifying Juliet's related feelings by emphatically continuing, "and all disguise was disgusting to her, if not induced by the most imperious necessity" (773). During the New Forest episodes, she is directly and aggressively hunted and thus requires extreme means of preservation, which in this case come in the form of overt disguise and performance of alternate identities. The period during which she is known as "Ellis," however, lacks this intensity of danger, as she is not directly pursued and so has no need to resist her native disgust for disguise in overtly disguising herself in either appearance or demeanor. Thus, Juliet's repulsion towards theatrical performance can still indicate the unlikelihood that she would willingly construct and socially perform the alter-identity of "Ellis" under such circumstances for such an extended period of time.

Instead, the role of Ellis seems to be created and enacted upon Juliet by the other characters, made "real" by their performative actions of believing the Ellis identity to be true and subsequently behaving in accordance to their various conceptions of the character of Ellis that originate in their own speculation about the details of Juliet's background and identity. Their actions are performative in the sense that they "constitute [a] reality through their performance," that reality consisting of what theorist Judith Butler calls the "constructed identity…the performative accomplishment which the mundane social audience…comes to believe and [subsequently] to perform the mode of belief" (Bial 145). By conceiving of the character that they call "Ellis" and by identifying it as part of a specific social class (lower upper class or upper middle class), the characters have thus constructed the "Ellis" identity, believe that it is real, and thus constitute it as reality through their behaving as if it were real.

Because the "Ellis" identity can thus be viewed as constructed and perpetuated by characters external to Juliet, analysis of that identity actually reflects more about the preoccupations and views of those characters rather than about Juliet. This is so because those who call her by that name inevitably treat Juliet according to their conception of the "Ellis" figure, allowing those assumptions to dictate and guide their behavior towards and around her according to established social convention. Significantly, once Juliet is given the name of "Ellis," a name by which others can refer to her, almost all of the characters display a greater comfort and willingness to interact with her. This seems to be partly because, along with the establishment of the name "Ellis," they have collectively established her as belonging to a particular social class, thus allowing them to conceive more clearly how to treat her. Coinciding with the establishment of the "Ellis" name, the speculation about Juliet's background and identity that is fueled by suspicious characters is never fully extinguished but is narrowed to a relatively small body of tentative marking possibilities. Almost all of the main characters identify her as most likely being, as the elite Mrs. Howel does, "but a dependant…[to] be smiled or frowned upon at will" (Burney 121). Even the servants participate in this conjecture, as betrayed by the familiar behavior of one of Mrs. Howel's female servants, who "follow[s]…Ellis to the breakfast-room, and seating herself upon a sofa, [begins] a discourse with the freedom of addressing a disgraced dependent" (136). In this implicit consensus that is reached among this particular set of characters about this foundational characteristic of "Ellis," her social class, the Ellis identity is thus further developed and placed upon Juliet, transforming her in the interpretative understandings of those with whom she lives, socializes, and works in Brighthelmstone, and, in the understanding of the reader who also remains ignorant of Juliet's true identity and name at this point in the narrative. Importantly, it must be noted that these circumstances exist not necessarily as the result of Juliet's deliberate performance of that identity and its attendant social class.

    The assertion that Juliet does not deliberately perform the alter-identity of Ellis can also be supported by the evidence in her repeated and sustained refusals to name herself and reluctance to even appear in public social situations during the time that she is known as Ellis. Occurring frequently, this circumstance is perhaps most succinctly noted by Harleigh, who explains early on that "her wish of concealment is open and confessed" (34). Such behavior and concerns show a resistance to performing, even inadvertently, the Ellis identity in its resistance to placing herself before an audience for whom she would perform. As influential performance theorist Erving Goffman has established, "'performance' [is defined] as a framing arrangement which plays a circumscribed sequence of activity before persons in an 'audience' role, whose duty it is to observe at length the activities of the 'performers' without directly participating in those activities," or, in other words, is understood as "'cultural behavior for which a person assumes responsibility to an audience'" (Carlson 38). Since Juliet thus needs an audience in order to perform, her avoidance of that audience suggests that she avoids performance altogether. Further, she is often pressed to appear in public by various characters. The actions of others that press and ultimately force Juliet to submit herself to the gaze of an audience may indicate further the ways in which others help to create and perpetuate the identity of "Ellis"; forcing her to appear in public allows them to enact their performative actions, manifested in their treatment of and interactions with her, that "make real" the Ellis identity.

Juliet, then, can be seen metaphorically as a blank slate, or "tabula rasa," which, suggestively, the *Oxford English Dictionary* defines as meaning "scraped tablet" in direct translation from the original Latin, and in definition, "a tablet from which the writing has been erased, and which is therefore ready to be written upon again; a blank tablet". This applies very evocatively to this circumstance, as Juliet, by her own initial refusals to name herself and provide any details about her true identity and background, thus metaphorically "scrapes clean" her identity as far as it is understood in the interpretative contexts of those whom she encounters in Brighthelmstone. In committing this metaphorical "scraping," Juliet thus renders herself a "tabula rasa" on which the characters with whom she interacts metaphorically inscribe onto her person a new identity, one that they have named "Ellis" and ascribed the characteristics of a working class single young woman. When viewed in this way, the interpretative possibility becomes clear that the "Ellis" identity is actually created, professed, and perpetuated not by Juliet but by the performative actions committed by those who surround her in Brighthelmstone. That Juliet does not participate in creating, perpetuating, or consciously performing the "Ellis" identity but instead merely provides others with a passive blank figure on which she allows them to place a name and accompanying identity and subsequently treat her according to their own interpretations is, then, a clear deductive possibility.

Yet this idea that Juliet does not consciously perform the Ellis identity or participate in its creation and perpetuation remains complicated and ambiguous. In fact, the very passivity that she adopts when others name her "Ellis" and treat her according to their conceptions of that identity could be interpreted as performative in itself, a paradox in which her lack of action operates as a deliberate repressive action. One scholar views Juliet's passivity in these circumstances as purposeful actions designed to disguise herself, stating that when "one of Juliet's acquaintances… assigns her the name of Ellis…Juliet accepts this mistake willingly, because it prevents her from committing the 'deceit' of designating a name for herself," thus interpretively transforming her lack of denial of the "Ellis" name as an act of acceptance (Anderson 439). Her actions during this period, as well, can be interpreted as her deliberate performance of this identity, especially its social class status. As noted earlier, there is not a single instance in the text where Juliet openly protests being known to others as "Ellis" or being treated as others have conceived of that identity. There are, however, several instances in which she is shown to repress indignant reaction to characters that treat her as they conceive of the "Ellis" working class identity. The exceedingly class-conscious Mrs. Maple, among others, consistently treats her without the respect due to one of her true class. When her repressive behavior is noted by Harleigh, who upon the occasion of her being sent to the home of Lady Howel to visit Lady Aurora, says to her "'How happy, how relieved...will you feel in obtaining, at last, a little reprieve from the narrow prejudice which urges this cruel treatment!'" (Burney 113). In her response, Juliet openly acknowledges her repressive efforts, imploring to him, "'You must not encourage me to resentment...but rather bid me, as I bid myself, when I feel it rising, subdue it by recollecting my strange—indefinable situation in this family!'" (113). In thus repressing her natural behavior and replacing it with seeming acceptance, Juliet can be said to perform as others expect "Ellis" would act, thus placing some responsibility on her for perpetuating it as a deceptive disguise of her true personal identity.

These repressive actions are also joined by more overt ones that can similarly be interpreted as part of Juliet's overt efforts to perform the personal identity of "Ellis." Driven by necessity, she accepts work as a seamstress, first through acceptance of piecework and finally through employment in a milliner's shop, and then as a teacher of the harp, both occupations suited to a member of the lower and middle classes. Her work in the milliner's shop perhaps most directly suggests that she performs the social class aspect of the Ellis identity as the condition of its spectacle is emphasized. Needing to earn money so that she can continue to rent her lodgings above Mrs. Matson's milliner's shop, Juliet requests piecework from her and, when she receives it, "beg[s] leave to return with it to her chamber," in response to which Mrs. Matson "stare[s] [at her] as if she had made a demand the most preposterous, and [tells her] that, if she meant to enter into business, she must be at hand to receive directions, and to learn how it should be done," thus meaning that she must do her work while seated behind the public counter of the busy shop (425-426).

In keeping with her reluctance to be seen in public, Juliet recoils at the possibility of working out in the open, but, as the narrator explains, "to enter into business was far from the intention of Juliet; but the fear of dismission, should she proclaim how transitory were her views, silenced her into acquiescence; and she seated herself behind a distant counter" where "perforce, she was initiated into a new scene of life" and "the starers were happy to present themselves where there was something to see" (426, 429-430). Juliet's revulsion to thus placing herself as a spectacle of lower middle class service is emphasized more emphatically later on, when she gains similar employment at a different milliner's establishment, but where she can work in private, "no longer constrained to remain in an open shop, in opposition to her inclinations and her wishes of concealment; no longer startled by the continual entrance and exit of strangers; nor exposed to curious enquirers, or hardy starers" (452). The continual emphasis that, during the execution of this type of work in public, she is framed as a spectacle of lower middle class identity strongly suggests that Juliet thus implicitly performs that aspect of the Ellis identity since her audience accepts and notices her as doing so, thus confirming their understandings of her as a member of the working class. These actions are not framed as done with the intention to perpetuate the Ellis identity, but in doing them, Juliet does not deny the markers of that identity that others have created and placed upon her. In this way, her behavior can be viewed as akin to her overt performances of alter-identities mentioned previously, in which she acts in order to manipulate and preserve the assumptions of others and to thus to obtain something for her own benefit, in this case, the employment that will yield her money to sustain suitable housing and provisions. Therefore, by not actively discouraging the creation and perpetuation of the Ellis identity, Juliet can be said to implicitly promote it and, thus, have a conscious and deliberate hand in performatively propagating it as reality.

Closely related to passivity, silence can also be viewed as performative in similar ways. Although Juliet is oftentimes surprised into silence or rendered incapable of utterance, there are frequent instances in which her silence is the result of a deliberate rhetorical choice. One transparent example occurs when Miss Bydel explicitly demands information from Juliet in a decidedly direct manner, stating to her, "'But pray tell me this one thing, child; what was the first motive of your going over the seas? And what might be the reason of your coming back gain in such an untowardly sort of manner? without any money, or any one to be accountable for your character?'" (214). In response, Juliet deliberately "[makes] no answer," reasoning, as the narrator explains, that "The obligations, however heavy of endurance, which led her to bear similar, and still more offensive examinations from Mrs. Maple, existed not here; and the compulsion of debts of that nature, could alone strengthen the patience, or harden the feelings of a generous spirit, to sustain so rude and unfeeling an inquisition" (214). In this instance, and the many others like it, silence, instead of existing as an absence of comment, operates as a comment in itself. As such, it forces ambiguity in the sense that it leaves interpretation entirely up to the speculation of the character or characters who comprise Juliet's audience in these instances, as well as that of the reader, who is doubly affected as the narrator remains silent as well, not allowing any definitive insight into the information that Juliet consciously withholds. This clearly occurs in the example just provided, in which the only narrative support that the reader receives only reveals Juliet's disgust at being questioned, not betraying any clue to the details that she defiantly withholds from Miss Bydel (214). Juliet, in choosing to remain silent and to thus create this interpretive ambiguity, invites the other characters to continue to inscribe her "blank slate" of a personal identity with further interpretations of the Ellis character, thus encouraging the continued performative action that makes that identity "real." By creating circumstances that manipulate and encourage such performative inscription, then, Juliet can be said to effectively participate in the performance and perpetuation of the Ellis identity.

Further revealing that Juliet's intentional silences are, in part, a rhetorical strategy by which she encourages the perpetuation of the Ellis identity is an instance that occurs late in the novel in which her thoughts are interpreted correctly (as Juliet's actual thoughts) by her audience. Embroiled in a heated exchange with Harleigh, the young man with whom she is in love and who loves her, she declares to him that she must refuse him, just as she must flee the Frenchman who claims to be her husband, having forced her into an illegal marriage (779). Harleigh, in response to her declaration that she must leave, emphatically says to her "'You fly us, then...both alike? You put us upon a par?,'" to which Juliet quickly responds "'No!...him I fly because I hate;—You—,'" thus rendering herself silent before she completes her statement (779). Her surprise and lack of control in the situation is highlighted by the narrator's following description, which explains: "The deep scarlet which mounted into her whole face finished the sentence; in defiance of a sudden and abrupt breaking off, that meant and hoped to snatch the unguarded phrase from comprehension" (779). Here, interestingly, her appearance is framed as communicative, as somehow "finish[ing] her sentence" (779). Reading this sign, Harleigh's interpretive process is further detailed, as the narrator continues,

> But Harleigh felt its fullest contrast; his hopes, his wishes, his whole soul completed it by You, because I love!—Not that he could persuade himself that Juliet would have used those words; he knew the contrary; knew that she would sooner thus situated expire; but such, he felt, was the impulse of her thoughts; such the consciousness that broke off her speech (779).

Juliet's utter embarrassment and horror at being thus correctly interpreted despite her silence is apparent, as the narrator continues:

> Utterly confounded herself, at the half-pronounced thought, thus inadvertently surprised from her, and thus palpably seized and interpreted, she strove to devize some term that might obviate dangerous consequences; but she felt her cheeks so hot, so cold, and again so hot, that she durst not trust her face to his observation (779).

This embarrassment seems to suggest, then, that Juliet expects and hopes for an alternate interpretation, one over which she would exercise more control and one that exists as different from her true thoughts and feelings. When viewed in a broader sense, this suggests that she might actually be consciously reliant upon being identified as other than her true self, in this case, as Ellis, the identity by which she has largely been known. Further, this suggests that she conceives and wishes this alter-identity to be a separate, obscuring, and disguising identity, one that will both hide her true thoughts and emotions and offer figurative mask in their stead.

Earlier in the novel, there exists further and more specific evidence that supports this idea that Juliet views and intentionally uses her silence as a sort of disguise. This instance occurs in another interaction with Harleigh during which she ardently refuses his proffered advice that she decline to submit herself to the disgrace of performing on stage by giving a musical concert in order to earn money. He entreats her, not the first time, for a revelation of her true identity and background, pleading: "'Confide to me your name—your situation—the motives to your concealment—the causes that can induce such mystery of appearance, in one whose mind is so evidently the seat of the clearest purity,'" capping his considerable demand by directly mentioning her efforts to hide such details, directly calling those efforts "'a disguise'" (340). Instead of denying this injunction that her silence enacts a sort of disguise, Juliet concedes that it does act in such a manner, stating "'Disguise, I acknowledge, Sir, you may charge me with'" (340). Yet she qualifies her confession, declaring that he may not accuse her of treachery, continuing, "'but not deceit! I give no false colouring. I am only not open'" (340). Interestingly, Harleigh immediately acquiesces, asserting "'That, that is what first struck me as a mark of a distinguished character! That noble superiority to all petty artifices, even for your immediate safety; that undoubting innocence, that framed no precautions against evil constructions; that innate dignity, which supported without a murmur such difficulties, such trials;—'" (340). When closely examined, then, Juliet seems to wield her silence as a rhetorical disguise, but not with the intent to deceive, but, instead, to only obscure. This is inherently problematic, since disguise, by providing a false front, does deceive those who encounter it. But Juliet's conviction that she does not intend to overtly deceive others by being, as she states, "not open" suggests that she views her actions as only providing others the opportunity to create impressions of her that are not actually created by herself. She therefore essentially denies any agency in creating and perpetuating any false identity, specifically that of Ellis, the one by which she is known and understood during both of these particular scenes.

Juliet further denies her active participation in creating and perpetuating the Ellis identity when she also goes so far as to deny agency in withholding the details about her true identity and background soon after the remarks made during the previously mentioned scene occur. As the conversation continues with Harleigh's anguished lament that he must be shut out of the knowledge of her true identity, Juliet replies that she is powerless to provide him with the information, declaring "' my confidence I cannot give you; it is out of my power'" (341). This avowal is final, as she subsequently ignores Harleigh's further protests and demands of him that he "'persecute [her] no longer!'" before ordering his departure (341-342). By thus denying agency in her decisions to remain silent when pressed for personal information, Juliet tangentially denies agency in overtly disguising herself from others, placing the blame for the creation and maintenance of her disguise squarely on the actions of others. Undoubtedly, then, the issue of whether or not Juliet consciously performs the Ellis identity remains provokingly ambiguous throughout the novel.

Gesture is also framed as being capable of significant communication, and as such, closely tied with silence as it has been discussed here. That the power of gesture as a form of meaningful language was emphasized greatly during the eighteenth century is clear, as noted by prominent novelist Samuel Richardson, who had stated "Silence indeed to me is a Commendation…For Air and Attention, and Non-Attention, as Occasions require, will show Meaning beyond what Words can; to the Observing" (qtd. in McKillop 90)[3]. Similar assertions can be found in the writings of prominent rhetorical lecturer Thomas Sheridan, who, in his work on elocutionary method, "asserts the centrality of the 'language of emotions,'" by "praising the natural language of tones and gesture as the most powerful aspect of elocution" (Spoel 89).[4] These ideas are clearly derived from Cicero's On the Ideal Orator (55 B.C.), in which he asserts that in order to achieve most effective communication, "…emotions ought to be accompanied by gestures—not those used on the stage, which depict the individual words, but gestures that indicate the content and the ideas as a whole, not by imitating them, but by signifying them" (294). Though Sheridan clearly deals with spoken oratory, his principles significantly affected the writing of literature during the period, including, notably, the ways in which gesture is framed in

---

[3] Richardson's statement originally appeared in a letter he had written to Miss Sophia Westcomb (McKillop 90).
[4] Spoel uses Sheridan's A Course of Lectures on Elocution (1762) for her study on his rhetorical teachings.

The Wanderer. In several instances, Juliet's gestures stand in place of oral assertions as a form of meaningful communication; yet because of the lack of words used during these instances, the meaning of her gestures is left entirely to the interpretation of the viewer. Perhaps the most vivid example occurs during the episode in which Juliet is captured by the Frenchman who claims to be her husband. Horror-stricken by the assertion that Juliet is married and has eloped from her husband, Harleigh begs for any form of communication from her as she is forcefully led from him, imploring to her "'Speak, Madam, speak! Utter but a syllable!—Deign only to turn towards me!—Pronounce but with your eyes that he has no legal claim…" (Burney 729). In response, Juliet provides no words but expresses communicative gesture, as the narrator relates "She clapped her hands upon her forehead, in an action of despair; but the word was not spoken,--not a syllable was uttered! A look, however, escaped her, expressive of a soul in torture, yet supplicating his retreat" (729). In addition to employing the oratorical ideas of Cicero and Sheridan, Burney also seems to emphasize Cicero's further emphasis upon the face, and particularly the eyes, as the instrument that "should be used to signify our feelings in a way suited to the actual type of our speech" (294). This places gesture in a similar state to that of silence, in that each allows the audience, which is constituted in this particular case by Harleigh, to construct meanings for Juliet's communicative actions and to respond accordingly, thus acting performatively in perpetuating the Ellis identity as reality. This ultimate responsibility and freedom of the audience to thus interpret meaning is further accentuated by the circumstance that, oftentimes, when gesture stands as the only form of communication happening in a given instance, omniscience is lacking, as the narrator fails to provide insight into Juliet's true thoughts and intentions as in this case. Compounding this is that omniscience is also absent in relation to the interpretations and subsequent actions of Juliet's audience; the narrator, in most instances, provides neither approval nor condemnation of any interpretation or responsive action as made either correctly or incorrectly responsive to Juliet's true thoughts and intentions. In this sense, it can never be clear whether Juliet's communicative gestures are made as deliberate performances consciously designed to assert the Ellis identity as neither the characters who comprise her audience nor the reader is allowed the ability to distinguish them as indicative of her true thoughts and personal identity or not. By narratively withholding this ability from the characters and the reader, Burney seems to highlight the ambiguities inherent in such interpretive situations.

  Another problematic aspect is the recognition of Juliet's true identity, that of a person of the upper echelons of British society—no other than the legitimate daughter of Lord Granville—by her half-siblings Lady Aurora Granville and Lord Melbury, by her suitor, Albert Harleigh. Throughout the narrative, from the beginnings of their respective acquaintances with Juliet, each of these individual characters resists the popular recognition of Juliet as a member of the working class. Though they refer to her as "Ellis," they develop and retain the belief that the accoutrements of the Ellis identity, particularly its ascribed social class, are not true, but are, in fact, gross inaccuracies that betray the unkind propensities of the other characters to feed on scandal and to elevate their own status through the ridicule of another placed lower than themselves on the social continuum. This recognition of Juliet's actual social class is developed through the apprehension of qualities that are treated as innate. Lady Aurora and her brother Lord Melbury intuitively recognize that Juliet is of their class, as Aurora recognizes "the quick intelligence, the graceful manners, the touching sense of kindness, and the rare accomplishments" that she possesses, while Melbury soon after insists that others treat her "with the respect which he was sure her due" (118, 147). Harleigh repeatedly asserts his own apprehensions of Juliet's superior qualities, both learned and innate, as the narrator explains "To him, her language, her air, and her manner, pervading every disadvantage of apparel, poverty, and subjection, had announced her, from the first, to have received the education, and to have lived the life of a gentlewoman" and as later, he states himself,

> I think her...an elegant and well bred young woman, under some extraordinary and inexplicable difficulties: for there is a modesty in her air which art, though it might attain, could not support; and a dignity in her conduct in refusing all succour but [Elinor's], that make it impossible for me to have any doubt upon the fairness of her character (75).

All of these qualities are communicated through appearance and gesture, never explicit declaration or communication of fact. These displays demonstrate particular refined sensibilities, knowledge and practices that are viewed as limited to those of the upper class, of which an unerring exhibition of delicacy is perhaps most emphasized. Since these qualities are apparent to these characters, it can be argued that Juliet does not, in fact, perform according to the preconceived alter-identity of Ellis; if she were, she would certainly attempt to abandon such contrary markers.

On the other hand, however, one could also argue that this does not necessarily prove that Juliet unconsciously performs the part of Ellis. If adopting this view, one could claim that Juliet does perform the part of Ellis, whose foundational characteristic is that she belongs to a lower social class, and that the performance is merely flawed in that it cannot fully obscure Juliet's true identity and its attendant qualities. This view is also suggested by careful examination of the scenes in which Juliet, as Ellis, performs as Lady Townly in the drawing room theatrical production of The Provoked Husband. During this performance, Juliet enthralls the audience members with her emotive abilities, ironically revealing both her innate superiorities of sensibility and delicacy, qualities that are clearly delineated through the discourse of the novel as natural and indicative of belonging to the upper class, while simultaneously proving her talent as an actress (95-97). Immediately following her performance, in which her "nature" is emphasized as displayed, her "truly elevated carriage and appearance" are noted by even the most negatively prejudiced members of the audience (95-97). The implications of this circumstance, then, clearly suggest that Juliet may deliberately perform the alter-identity of Ellis in her everyday life and that her innate qualities show through that social performance just as they do when she skillfully performs the theatrical role of Lady Townly.

Perhaps the most compelling suggestion that Juliet acts deliberately and consciously as Ellis is when her true situation is revealed to Harleigh, and simultaneously, as I will show, to the reader. Encountering Juliet, who has been captured by the Frenchman who claims to be her husband, Harleigh is told by that man that she is a married woman, one who has run away from him and her marital obligations (727). Harleigh is considerably shocked and angry at this claim, at first vehemently denying the charges leveled against Juliet, then demanding that the man "'give an account of [him]self'" and declaring that he will "'defend that lady from [his] inhuman grasp, to the last drop of [his] blood!'" (728). Throughout the intense scene in which Harleigh and the Frenchman argue over her, Juliet remains silent and purely submissive, much to Harleigh's dismay, as he hopes she will deny the man's unflattering claims. Finally, he demands direct acknowledgement from her that the man's seemingly-outlandish claims are true, exhorting to her, "Speak, Madam, speak! Utter but a syllable!—Deign only to turn towards me!—Pronounce but with your eyes that he has no legal claim…Speak!—turn!—look but a moment this way!—One word! one single word!—'" (729). Instead of giving him the response that he longs to hear, Juliet "clapped her hands upon her forehead, in an action of despair," and confirms his fears, as the narrator describes: "but the word was not spoken—not a syllable was uttered! A look, however, escaped her, expressive of a soul in torture, yet supplicating his retreat" (729). She is then quickly and willingly locked into an adjoining room and thus moved out of the sight of Harleigh by the Frenchman (729). The narrator then relates in detail Harleigh's wretched reaction, stressing his disillusionment, in the following explanation:

> Harleigh now appeared to be lost! The violence of his agitation, while he concluded her to be wrongfully claimed, was transformed into the blackest and most indignant despondence, at her unresisting, however wretched acquiescence, to commands thus brutal; emanating from an authority of which, however evidently it was deplored, she attempted not to controvert the legality. The dreadful mystery, more direful than it had been depicted, even by the most cruel of his apprehensions, was now revealed: she is married! he internally cried; married to the vilest of wretches, whom she flies and abhors,—yet she is married! indisputably married! and can never, never,— even in my wishes, now be mine! (730).

The most obvious implication of this passage is that Juliet is revealed to Harleigh, as well as to the reader, as likely to be less virtuous that she originally seemed to both. This clear suggestion is severely disorienting to both Harleigh and the reader, as no omniscience is allowed; in fact, this is the only instance in the novel during which both Harleigh and the reader are separated from Juliet—neither can see her, know what is happening to her, or understand what she is thinking. This disorientation leads to a profound questioning and doubting of one's own perceptive abilities, both in Harleigh's conception of himself and in the reader's own experience. Each interpreter of Juliet's character, including Harleigh and the reader, is allowed by the narrator, who remains largely absent, to believe that he has been deceived, as if the character of Juliet has been partly hidden from the reader by the narrator and from the other characters by her own deceptive actions. Thus, the reader is allowed to experience the same self-doubt and disoriented questioning of previous interpretations as does Harleigh, creating a profound instance of metanarrative effect. This intriguing merging of perspective is further established by the subtle yet profound shift in narrative perspective during the above-mentioned passage. Indicated by the deft use of the colon in the phrase "The dreadful mystery, more direful than it had been depicted, even by the most cruel of his apprehensions, was now revealed: she is married!," the prose shifts from the third person perspective of the narrator to that of Harleigh, who is allowed to vent his dismay and anguish in the first person (730). This shift occurs almost imperceptibly to the reader who is likely, at this point, to be so engrossed in the emotional drama so vividly depicted in the passage and to follow its manipulative rhetorical shift unthinkingly. By thus adopting and continuing from the viewpoint of Harleigh at this crucial moment in the narrative, Burney effectively merges their interpretive experiences of Juliet, resolutely suggesting that they both have, perhaps, been fooled by a deceitful and talented actress.

Of course, it eventually comes to light that Juliet, though she does hide her past, is not as corrupt as she may seem during that particular scene. She is effectively pardoned later on when it is discovered that what the Frenchman claims to be her legal marriage was in fact forced and illegal, thus proving her virtue to be intact (753). But Harleigh, along with the reader, is left with a distinct uncertainty about these conditions for a significant period of time. This effectively creates a sense of betrayal in both, allowing the possibility that both have been purposefully deceived, Harleigh by Juliet and the reader by the narrator. This sense of the possible perfidy of

Juliet is allowed to continue long enough that both Harleigh and the reader are placed in potential opposition to her, creating a sense of disorientation. In fact, the interpretive authority of both Harleigh and the reader are thus called into question, subordinating each to the control of Juliet and the narrator respectively, marking each as an outsider, Harleigh to Juliet's confidence and the reader to the text itself. Paradoxically, however, these circumstances simultaneously draw both further into the interests of the one who exerts such control over him, as Harleigh becomes increasingly intent on accessing confirmative information from Juliet and the reader is drawn further into his investment and engagement with the text which is controlled through the creation of suspense and attendant doubt by the equally furtive narrator.

Clearly, with so many contradictory interpretations possible, it remains decidedly ambiguous whether Juliet deliberately performs the Ellis identity with the intent to calculatingly deceive those with whom she comes into contact or whether that identity and the assumptions that shape it are truly created, professed and perpetuated by others who are overeager to identify the nameless woman to enable their interaction with and self-interested manipulation and use of her. In creating such problematic ambiguity, Burney achieves significantly experimental effects in the creation of third person narration which explores simultaneously issues of personal identity and its relation to performance and performativity in provocative and complex ways. Allowing oneself as a reader to carefully explore the details of the narrative is thus significantly rewarding in that it reveals those intricacies and thus resists reductive or broad readings that may threaten to obscure Burney's narrative and theoretical innovations.

That the issue of whether Juliet consciously performs the alter-identity of Ellis throughout much of The Wanderer with the intent to disguise her true identity and to deceive others for purposes of personal gain is treated within the narrative in a strikingly ambiguous manner has been made clear. Such ambiguity seems appropriate, though, when the narrative situations are viewed in context with various philosophical debates that, though begun much earlier than the composition and publication of The Wanderer in 1814, persisted throughout eighteenth-century British thought, and more importantly, in its contemporary writings, both fictional and essayistic. Throughout this novel, Burney seems to engage several philosophical issues. Most striking are those that concern the nature of personal identity; it is these that are so closely tied to the issues of performance and performativity that generate such arresting ambiguity throughout much of the narrative.

As noted by several scholars, the idea that personal identity exists in consciousness rather than in substance is universally accepted today, but it once was a rather radical notion, one that threatened "the old theological concept of the self-as-substance" and thus, the basis for many arguments involving morality and personal responsibility (Fox 4). As Kathryn J. Ready, quoting Felicity A. Nussbaum's work entitled The Autobiographical Subject: Gender and Ideology in Eighteenth-Century England, states, "'The historical period of eighteenth-century England…is a time when identity and character are in particular crisis,' allowing the emergence of 'nonhegemonic concepts about the self as well as new hegemonies in formation'" (565). All conjecture about the nature of personal identity during this time is based in the philosophical assertions of John Locke, who presented groundbreaking ideas in his Essay Concerning Human Understanding (1690; 1694). In this treatise, Locke defines "personal identity" as "the sameness of a rational Being," claiming that "as far as this consciousness can be extended backwards to any past Action or Thought, so far reaches the Identity of that Person; it is the same self now it was then, and 'tis by the same self with this present one that now reflects on it, that that Action was done" (106). This groundbreaking assertion that the self remains the same throughout time due to the circumstance that it is constituted in consciousness is further complicated by Locke, who goes on to state that "personal identity consists, not in the identity of Substance but...in the Identity of Consciousness," and that "Nothing but consciousness can unite remote Existences into the same Person, the Identity of Substance will not do it" (110-111). These ideas provided fertile fodder for eighteenth-century philosophical debate, especially since, as Christopher Fox notes,

> By severing personal identity from substantial identity, [eighteenth-century thinkers argued] that Locke had left consciousness in no recognizable relation to that substance of which it was supposed to be a mode. And even more dangerously, by questioning our ability to know the soul, Locke had brought its very existence into question and, as some were to argue, had opened the door to a totally materialistic interpretation of the self (13-14).

In shifting the notion of where personal identity originates and is perpetuated, Locke threw eighteenth-century debate about the nature of the self into vigorous conjecture.

The most notable participants in the eighteenth-century debate about the nature of the self and how it relates to identity and, more specifically, to Locke's assertions about the subject include Joseph Butler and David Hume. The main debate can be broken into two interrelated overarching concerns: the concept of the self-in-consciousness and the idea of a continuous or abiding self, one that remains what one can refer to and conceive of as the "same person" over the course of time and throughout the inevitable changes that may occur over that period of time. Butler, in the first appendix of his larger piece The Analogy of Religion (1736), entitled Of Personal Identity, in which he "explicitly react[s] to the 'strange perplexities' about 'the meaning of…identity' which Locke's theories had raised," claims "that 'personality' is indeed 'permanent' and is made so by 'substance'" (Fox 7). Therefore, Butler argues "against the Lockean concept of the self-in-consciousness," claiming instead "that the personality is instead a 'permanent' entity and is made so by 'substance'" (8). Writing later, David Hume, in his A Treatise of Human Nature (1739-1740), accepts Locke's idea that personal identity lies in consciousness instead of material substance but, as Kathryn J. Ready explains, "he takes another bold step in daring to question the existence of immaterial substance, controversially maintaining that the soul is most likely a human invention," thus "exacerbat[ing] the worst fears of opponents to the theory of self-in-consciousness by developing its most troubling implications" (564). These philosophical theories were also debated within the literary realm, as personages such as Alexander Pope and Joseph Addison creatively addressed and explored related ideas in poetry and essay. Clearly, as the issue of the nature of personal identity and the self was a point of serious and wide-ranging contention throughout the eighteenth-century, it is certainly unsurprising that novelists, such as Burney, drew it into their works, thus entering the larger philosophical conversation.

It can, in fact, be said that Burney engages these issues in all four of her published novels, as all deal primarily with a young woman protagonist who spends the narrative undergoing trials of experience and coming-of-age, and in a sense, growing into her more mature and seemingly inevitable place as an established married woman. Throughout the various protagonists' trials, traits that are treated as innate to their various personalities, such as sensibility and delicacy, are highlighted, demonstrating, in one sense, that the ultimate trials that these young women face involve the careful maintenance of their virtuous personal identities during times in which it is often tempted, tested, and even directly assaulted. In The Wanderer, similar issues do appear, but the specific issues of the nature of personal identity as discussed by John Locke and then by eighteenth-century philosophers seem also to be engaged in particularly experimental and profound ways. Just as issues of performance and performativity are raised, tested and challenged in this novel in order to expose crucial attendant ambiguities, so are the issues of personal identity, specifically that of the concept of the self-in-consciousness and the related debate over the questioned concept of a "same self," or an abiding self that persists as continuous across time. Once again, in displaying these issues through the various episodes of the narrative, Burney seems to never imply a definitive statement about the issue at hand, but instead raises provocative ambiguities that force the reader to consider the complexities of the bewildering debate.

Not surprisingly, both of the major theoretical lines of the issue of the eighteenth-century debate surrounding the nature of personal identity are engaged most directly in The Wanderer and, more specifically, in circumstances that surround Juliet. As discussed previously, considerable ambiguity exists in the matter of Juliet's personal identity, especially since her true identity is seemingly obscured throughout most of the novel by the fact that it is not revealed until the latter quarter of the narrative and because she is referred to by a multitude of proper and descriptive names at various times. Despite these circumstances, however, it clearly can be argued that Juliet's true identity is constantly present and deftly referred to throughout the narrative as those qualities that are treated as innate to her personality remain constant no matter how she is understood and identified by the characters with which she interacts or how she is portrayed to the reader by the provokingly manipulative narrator. Because these innate qualities remain consistently present from the very opening of the narrative to its close, Burney seems to suggest that Juliet unerringly retains the same distinct personality, no matter what she is referred to in name, because she remains conscious of her own true identity.

That Juliet consistently retains a determined focus of her true self and, importantly, those qualities crucial to her personality—virtue, delicacy, and sensibility—is often emphasized through the narrative. Throughout the novel, Burney allows Juliet to retain these bastions of what is figured as her innate personality, traits that are portrayed as basic and constant to her character. Further emphasizing their innate quality, they fully emerge once Juliet appears as herself at the close of the narrative, as she is no longer framed by the alternative identity of Ellis. No longer known by any other name than her own and her past having been aired to all, she becomes known to all by her rightful name of Juliet Granville and, significantly, as a person fully in possession of those superior innate qualities. Her unaltered basic state is underscored by the acceptance she receives from Harleigh, Aurora, and Lord Melbury, who are simultaneously justified in their previous convictions of those personal characteristics, as well as those concerning her true social class and filial relationship. The idea of Juliet's true nature is also emphasized throughout the novel by the narrator, who allows the reader to see the basic qualities of Juliet throughout the narrative, equally throughout the time during which she is known as Ellis and throughout episodes of crisis and attendant deliberate disguise, including the flight scenes through the New Forest and even soon after she appears on the boat in the very beginning of the novel. These narrative comments, along with the episodic circumstances, when viewed in relation to the contemporary philosophical debates that either deny or affirm the Lockean notion that personal identity rests in consciousness rather than in material substance, become undoubtedly essential to accessing the novel's philosophical dimension. On one hand, they clearly depict, through example, that personality, as constitutive of personal identity, and the innate qualities that comprise its foundation, do indeed rest in the consciousness of an individual, as Juliet seems to remain as "Juliet" throughout the narrative because of her own consciousness of that identity. She is able to retain the same essential personal identity throughout the narrative, despite the fact that she is called by several proper names at various times and even assumes several different physical appearances, simply because she is always consciously aware of herself as Juliet. Furthermore, these circumstances also seem to corroborate the philosophical idea of the abiding self; Juliet, throughout all changes in name, external appearance, and situation, is shown to retain the same personal identity. When viewed in this manner, then, Burney seems to figuratively imply philosophical support for the concepts of self-in-consciousness and of the abiding, continuous self.

Though that philosophical statement is thus clearly suggested, the issue cannot be said to be portrayed as definitive or uncomplicated. Ambiguity is created with attendant episodic and narrative representations of opposing views, thus creating a complicated interaction of possibilities rather than straightforward argument. While the suggestion that personal identity does exist in consciousness is present through the portrayal of Juliet's seemingly unerring concept of her true personality, the question is raised about whether that identity is more true than those created by Juliet's outward appearances and behaviors that influence the consciousnesses and understandings of those whom she encounters and who thus construct and perpetuate her personal identity as that of "Ellis" with their subsequent performative behaviors towards her and actions committed around her. If one were to accept the interpretation that during the period in which Juliet is known as "Ellis" by those whom she encounters and that those characters, through their performative actions and belief in the "Ellis" identity thus constitute it as "reality," then it would follow that the Ellis identity operates as a true identity of Juliet for that period of time. It would do so because it exists as true in the consciousness of the individuals who create and perpetuate it, thus keeping with the Lockean notion of the existence of self-in-consciousness. If this is the case, then, it raises the philosophical possibility that Juliet exists as two separate personal identities equally during this period, that of Juliet and that of Ellis, as both exist as equally "real" in the consciousnesses of various individuals. Clearly, Burney, in creating this particularly complex narrative situation, raises several intriguing philosophical possibilities and ambiguities related to the issues of personal identity, performance, and performativity.

Similarly, just as it has been shown that the narrative circumstances surrounding Juliet can be said to imply the acceptance of the existence of the abiding self, when examined further, the text also seems to raise the opposing view as well, thus creating another point of implicit philosophical contention and ambiguity. Though it can be argued that because Juliet seemingly retains an unerring consciousness of her own personality, one that is grounded in the essential innate traits of virtue, delicacy, and sensibility, there are points in the novel that seem to suggest that the character of Juliet does undergo substantial change in personality and, thus, personal identity, becoming a slightly different character over the span of the narrative. Perhaps this is most plainly suggested by the scenes of flight that occur through the New Forest. This decidedly Gothic series of episodes seems to have captivating allusions and roots in the highly imaginative works of Edmund Spenser, especially his masterwork The Faerie Queene (1590, 1596), a text that was widely read and loved throughout eighteenth-century Britain. Throughout that work, the forest, as it has operated in countless pieces of literature and folklore, symbolizes, on one level, an area of danger. Metaphorically, the journey into and through the forest can also come to symbolize a period of deep personal change or crisis during which one undergoes intense personal metamorphosis. In The Wanderer, the New Forest is, indeed, depicted as a place of shadowy dangers, many of which take Juliet by surprise and even several that she is unable to completely ascertain and comprehend in an immediate fashion, requiring her to go through periods of disorientation and ignorance before she eventually learns the true nature of the menaces that she faces. Perhaps the most striking example occurs when she lodges in the cottage of what turns out to be a poacher (678-683). During her stay, she witnesses the dumping of what she believes to be the human body of "some victim to murderous rapacity," her fears confirmed when she sees "a large clot of blood on the floor" nearby (682). Fearing for her life, as she incorrectly interprets the owners of the cottage to be murderers, she runs away, only to discover the truth of their crime much later (683-684). Repetitions of this type of misinterpretation occur throughout the time she spends in the New Forest until she is rendered entirely disoriented and incapable of recognizing her surroundings, as indicated by her period of hazy recollection that is explained by the narrator:

> She wandered thus for some hours, now sinking into marshy ground, now wounded by rude stones, now upon a soft, smooth plain, and now stung or torn by bushes, nettles and briars; till she concluded it to be about midnight. A light wind then arose…and the moon, which, though upon the wane, afforded a gentle, melancholy light, shewed her that she was once again in the midst of the New Forest (704).

Such profound disorientation brought about by repeated terror can be seen to symbolically indicate a change in character.

Further symbolic of such a change, though she does retain the essential markers of her personal identity throughout these scenes, those being her virtue, delicacy, and sensibility, she does emerge, significantly, as unable to either perpetuate or be known according to the Ellis identity. In losing this option or ability, she also seems to lose the independence it allowed her. Without the Ellis identity, Juliet submits relatively easily to both her persecutors and to the characters that plague her to reveal her true identity, very unlike her previously spirited and seemingly impermeable resistance to submit to either. Because of these circumstances, the New Forest scenes seem to thus operate allegorically as do the forest scenes in previous literary works, notably Spenser's <u>The Faerie Queene</u>, serving to symbolize a deep crisis of and change in Juliet's personal identity, thus subtly contradicting the philosophical assertion of an abiding, unchanging self that endures throughout the passage of time. However, this interpretation, when viewed in relation to the insistent circumstances that suggest that she retains the essential vestiges of her true personality, cannot be considered as definitive; thus, Burney, in juxtaposing these suggestions, only exposes the troubling ambiguities that surround the related philosophical concepts that surround the notion of the abiding self.

Perhaps the most direct engagement of the philosophical debates related to the issues of personal identity that occurs in the novel does not, however, directly involve Juliet. In the latter third of the novel, following Juliet's escape from the Frenchman, Elinor bursts in upon her meeting with Harleigh in which he again professes his regard for her and she attempts to deny him, despite her own similar regard for him. For much of the narrative, Elinor, having directly professed her love for Harleigh and been rejected by him, threatens and attempts suicide, all in public and all in very theatrical ways. In this particular scene, she again expresses her intent to end her own life, though she demands a "last conference" with Harleigh in which she demands him to prove that she should not kill herself (780). Thus follows an extended episode in which Juliet is present, as she stands by the side of Elinor seemingly throughout the duration, but remains absolutely silent and drops from the narrative perspective until the conversation is concluded, when she "[comes] forward to support" a fainting Elinor (794). The episode stands out, not only because of its concentrated nature, consisting entirely of wordy dialogue, but because of its philosophical subject and solemn tone. In any reading, even a casual one, it is thus marked as odd in relation to the style of the rest of the narrative, but, when viewing the novel in relation to the contemporary debates about the nature of personal identity, it becomes obviously crucial to understanding the philosophical undercurrent of the text.

During this critical scene, Harleigh and Elinor engage in an impassioned debate over the nature of the self and how it relates to ideas of immortality and the soul, especially in the ways the conception of the soul affects religious concerns. Elinor, in the beginning and throughout most of the debate, argues that the self, or personal identity, is ultimately material. She views the soul, or the place in which personal identity rests, as an entity that exists separately from the material body, but argues that the soul and body are inextricably linked because the working of the material body allows the mind to create the consciousness wherein the soul lies, declaring in answer to Harleigh's questions of "'what, Elinor, is imagination? You will not call it a part of your body?'", that "'the blood which still circulates in our veins, Harleigh, gives imagination its power'" (789). She argues, then, that once the body ceases to work in death, the soul can no longer survive; therefore, she does not believe that there is immortality in the sense of an afterlife since the soul, without the consciousness that creates and perpetuates it, simply cannot exist in any sense. It is on this interpretation of Locke's concept of the self-in-consciousness that her intent to commit suicide lies. She figures that, since there cannot be a continued existence of the soul after the death of the body, she will not face the punishments professed by Christianity that those who commit the sin of suicide are doomed to face in the afterlife, somewhat morbidly declaring "'is it not clear that death is an end to all? an abyss eternal? a conclusion? Nature comes but for succession; though the pride of man would give her resurrection. Mouldering all together we go, to form new earth for burying our successors'" (783). Interestingly, this very interpretation is one of the major ways in which Locke's ideas threatened the dominant theological principles of his day. Burney, in creating this situation and highlighting it in such a direct debate within her narrative, clearly thus directly engages the attendant contemporary philosophical debates of which she must have been very aware.

Elinor's views are extremely troubling to Harleigh, who openly rejects the idea that the soul, as the seat of personal identity, is inextricably tied to the working of the material body. He warns Elinor of her mistake, telling her,

> "Hasten not, Elinor, thence, to your favourite conclusion, that soul and body, if wearied or rested together, are, therefore, one and the same thing...All proves that the connexion between mind and body, however intimate, is not blended;—though where its limits begin, or where they end,—who can tell?" (791).

Instead, he asserts that the soul is a separate and unknowable entity that very likely can and does persist after the physical demise of the material body. Further, he insists to Elinor that her folly lies in her instance on having empirical evidence to prove the workings and existence of the soul. He passionately declares to her,

> "What know you of this soul which you settle to be so easily annihilated? By what criterion do you judge it? You have none! save a general consciousness, that a something there is within us that mocks all search, yet that always is uppermost; that anticipates good or evil; that outruns all events; that feels the blow ere the flesh is touched; that expects the sound before the ear receives it; that, unseen, untraced, unknown, pervades, rules, animates all! that harbours

>thoughts, feelings, designs which no human force can controul; which no mortal, unaided by our own will, can discover; and which no aid whatever, either of our own or of others, can bring forward to any possible manifestation!" (792).

Harleigh thus insists that there are some mysteries to life that one can never know for certain, further declaring to her "'Oh Elinor! mock not, but revere the impenetrable mystery of eternity! Ignorance is here our lot; presumption is our most useless infirmity'" (791). He also thus asserts to her that the state of being able to somehow know that the soul exists and that it is the seat of personal identity but to never be able to definitively know about it or understand its nature or workings through the examination of empirical evidence is no reason to reject the possibility—and hope— that it persists in an afterlife, thus ensuring the personal identity a sort of immortality.

Though both sides are argued with equal vehemence by both characters, Harleigh eventually prevails, finally convincing Elinor not that he is correct but that neither of them can claim to be right. By exposing the unknowable nature of the subject of the debate, being the soul or personal identity, he convinces Elinor that to decide to commit suicide based on an idea that cannot be proven to be true would be dangerous, causing her to exclaim rather suddenly, "'Oh Albert! conquering Albert! I hope,--I hope;--my soul may be immortal!'" before fainting into Juliet's arms (794). His lengthy final tirade that causes her sudden change of mind emphasizes not the correctness of his view of the soul as immortal but the very ambiguity of both of their views on question, as he declares to Elinor:

"Reflect only,—that the quality, that faculty, be its nature, its durability, and its purpose what they may, which the world at large agrees to call soul, has its universal comprehension from something that is felt; not that is proved! Yet who, and where is the Atheist, the Deist, the Infidel of any description, gifted with means to demonstrate, that, in quitting the body with the parting breath, it is necessarily extinct? that it may not, on the contrary, still BE, when speech and motion are no more? when our flesh is mingled with the dust, and our bones are dispersed by the winds? and BE, as while we yet exist, no part of our body, no single of our sense; never, while we seem to live, visible, yet never, when we seem to die, perishable? May it not, when, with its last sigh, it leaves the body, mingle with that vast expanse of air, which no instrument can completely analyse, and which our imperfect sight views but as empty space? may not it mount to upper regions, and enjoy purified bliss?...May not the uncumbered soul...be received in the Heaven of Heavens, where it is destined—not, Oh wretched idea!—to eternal sleep, inertness, annihilating dust;--but to life, to joy, to sweetest reminiscence, to tenderest re-unions, to grateful adoration, to intelligence never ending! Oh! Elinor! keep for ever in mind, that if no mortal is gifted to prove that this is true;—neither is any one empowered to prove that it is false!" (793-794).

Though this tirade forcefully portrays Harleigh's ideas of what the afterlife of the soul might be, he is careful to only suggest it as a possibility, instead choosing as his rhetorical emphasis the very indefiniteness of any assertion about the nature of the soul and, more specifically, what happens to it once the body has ceased to function. As Harleigh thus wins the debate depicted in this episode, as he is framed throughout the narrative as a character with which the reader is intended to relate, and as Elinor is equally consistently framed as an inherently unstable and even dangerous character, it can be argued that Harleigh's view is to be taken as the moral and philosophical statement of the novel. Yet that his professed final declaration rests on the assertion of the inarguable ambiguity and incomprehensible nature of the subject of the debate is undoubtedly significant, thus further emphasizing what seems as Burney's intent to expose the ambiguities of the nature of personal identity and its attendant philosophical issues without fully supporting ideas on either side of what was still, in the latter eighteenth-century, an ongoing debate.

Harleigh's final speech to Elinor also betrays a strong resemblance to ideas alluded to in an Oriental Tale published in Joseph Addison's popular publication The Spectator as entry number 578. Appearing in print on August 9, 1714, the tale "playfully juxtaposes John Locke's disembodied theory of personal identity, developed in his Essay Concerning Human Understanding (1690), with a Persian tale featuring the magical transmigration of souls from one body to another (Richardson 232).[5] That the tale directly addresses Locke's ideas is made apparent by its prefatory material, which begins "There has been very great Reason, on several

---

[5] Editor Alan Richardson goes on to note that this particular Oriental tale was seemingly popular throughout eighteenth-century Europe, explaining that "The tale (which may have been contributed by Addison's cousin, Eustace Budgell) was condensed from Ambrose Philips's Thousand and One Days: Persian Tales (1714), a translation of Francois Petis de la Croix's Les Mille et un jour: Contes Persans (1710-12). The same tale, or a close variant, was later adapted by the Italian dramatist Carlo Gozzi in his comedy Il Re Cervo (1762)" (232).

Accounts, for the learned World to endeavour at settling what it was that might be said to compose personal Identity," further grounding it in Locke's reasonings by condensing his views in the following explanatory manner:

> Mr. Lock[e], after having premised that the Word Person properly signifies a thinking intelligent Being that has Reason and Reflection, and can consider it self as it self; concludes That it is Consciousness alone, and not an Identity of Substance, which makes this personal Identity or Sameness...For as to this Point of being the same Self, it matters not whether this present Self be made up of the same or other Substances (233).

The tale, then, clearly engages both strains of the eighteenth-century philosophical debate that are addressed in The Wanderer, that of the concept of the self-in-consciousness and of the abject self.

The tale relates the story of King Fadlallah, the ruler of the Kingdom of Mousel who "ruled over his faithful Subjects for some time, and lived in great Happiness with his beauteous Consort Queen Zemroude," and who develops a quick and ardent admiration for a young man named Dervis, who he eventually becomes Falallah's "chief Companion and first Favourite" (234). Dervis soon shares with the prince that he has learned "the Power of re-animating a dead Body, by flinging [his] own Soul into it" from "an old Branchman" who he met during his travels in "the Indies" (234). He soon proves his mysterious skill by transferring his soul into the body of a deceased doe and then back to his own body, a feat he immediately and successfully convinces the prince to try himself (234-235). While the king's soul resides in the Doe, the conniving Dervis "shoot[s] his own Soul into the Royal Corps" and attempts to kill Falallah by shooting the doe in which his soul presently resides (235). His plan fails as the king, occupying the body of the doe, escapes the arrows leveled against him (235). The story continues as Dervis, in the body of the king, returns to "the Throne and Bed of the unhappy Fadlallah," thus taking the king's place by acting as him (235). During this time, the king transfers his soul into the body of a nightingale and becomes the queen's favorite pet (235-236). He continues in this state until Zemoroude's pet lapdog dies, when he "immediately found himself inclined to quit the shape of the Nightingale, and enliven this new Body," and successfully doing so (236). When the queen sees that her bird has died, she is excessively grieved; to calm her, "her Women immediately sent for the Dervis, to come and comfort her" (236). Highly concerned for her piteous state, the Dervis (who still inhabits the physical body of the king) promises her that "[her] Nightingale shall again revive every Morning and serenade you as before," responding to her bewildered disbelief by "[shooting] his Soul into the Nightingale" and thus reviving it for her to see (236). Seizing this opportunity, "the King, who was a Spectator of all that passed, lying under the Shape of a Lap Dog, in one Corner of the Room, immediately recovered his own Body, and running to the Cage with the utmost Indignation, twisted off the neck of the false Nightingale" (236). He then explains the entire story to the amazed Zemroude, proving its truth by recovering the dead body of Dervis (236).

Clearly, this fantastical tale is imbued with Locke's theories, engaging them in ways that suggest both experiment and warning. The inherent profession that both the king and Dervis retain the same personal identity throughout their transmigratory adventures implicitly asserts that physical substance has no bearing on that identity. Others may interpret that personal identity according to outward material appearances, as Zemroude, along with, apparently, the other inhabitants of the kingdom, accept Dervis as King Falallah simply because he appears as him in a physical sense. The same circumstances appear during the king's various physical transformations into the body of the nightingale and that of the lap dog. This clearly puts Locke's notion of the self-in-consciousness into practice while simultaneously arguing for his idea of the abiding self, as these examples also show that personal identity remains the same despite physical change and the changes that naturally occur in circumstance over time.

Thematic ties with The Wanderer are several, beginning most obviously with Juliet's transformations in physical appearance during which, as has been argued, she is shown to retain the vestiges of what is to be understood as the same essential personality. The most striking of these instances include her change in skin tone at the opening of the narrative, transforming in appearance from one with dark skin to one with a fair hue. The New Forest scenes, though involving less dramatic transformations of physical appearance, also display her ability to figuratively transform into different appearances through deliberate costuming, thus deceiving others into believing that she is someone who she is not. But also relevant is the tale's complex implications of the nature of the soul's existence. The tale clearly suggests that the soul, though distinct from the body, requires a physically functioning body in order to survive. This is shown through the circumstance that the king is able to end the existence of Dervis by killing the body of the nightingale in which his soul resides at the time of his death. This implication intersects significantly with the ideas of Elinor and Harleigh concerning the connection between the body and the soul, which is understood as the seat of personal identity, which are aired during their heated final debate. The Spectator story seems to support Elinor's view that the soul, while existing as distinct from the material body, requires a working physical body to create the consciousness in which it resides.

Beyond these two ways in which the ideas presented in the Oriental tale intersect with those presented in The Wanderer is perhaps a more significant undercurrent. Both narratives seem, in their complex experiments with Lockean ideas of the self, to betray a distinct anxiety surrounding the larger philosophical debate. Both seem to raise worry over the possibility that if one can only judge the individuals who surround him by relying on external appearance, but if true personal identity exists in the consciousness of an individual as an entity that can never be empirically viewed or understood, one cannot ever definitively know the true nature of his social interactions. This is clearly suggested in the circumstance related in the Oriental tale that the queen, believing that she is interacting with her husband during the time in which Dervis possesses his body, is, in a sense, committing adultery, a circumstance of which she becomes acutely aware, as betrayed by the ending, which depicts her as "so highly afflicted at the innocent Adultry in which she had for some time lived with the Dervis, that no Arguments even from Fadlallah himself could compose her Mind" (236). She eventually succumbs to her grief in death, "begging his Pardon with her last Breath for what the most rigid Justice could not have interpreted as a Crime" (236). A similar concern is shown throughout The Wanderer, first, with the continuously foregrounded concerns of the characters with which Juliet comes into contact throughout the narrative in which they express an unceasing need to know the details of her personal identity and background. More than just allowing them to interact with her more easily by putting her in a distinct social category, knowing Juliet's identity would alleviate the continual unease that they experience as the result of never being able to know with whom they are interacting. This particular anxiety is most vividly displayed during Harleigh's crisis of perception that he experiences when Juliet succumbs to her pursuers, seeming to admit through her actions that she is indeed a married woman who has been knowingly fleeing her lawful husband. His anguished self-doubt and disorientation most compellingly depicts the possible result of the crux of this particular anxiety, that of never being able to know the true nature of one's interactions with other individuals due to the unknowable state of the soul, in which rests personal identity, and the power and reliance that circumstance places on physical appearance, which in the related philosophical debates of the eighteenth century, may not have much congruence with one's true personal identity.

Also demonstrating this particular anxiety is the way in which Juliet's physical appearance is included in the narrative. Significantly, her true physical appearance in its entirety is not included until very late in the novel and after she has endured considerable danger during her flight through the New Forest and been rescued by Sir Jasper Harrington. Interestingly, her physical description comes from the flyer that announces the Frenchman's search for her, as read by Juliet herself. In it, she is described as "A young woman, tall, fair, blue-eyed; her face oval; her nose Grecian; her mouth small; her cheeks high coloured; her chin dimpled; and her hair of a glossy light brown" (756). Until this moment, the reader has only understood her appearance as one who has fair skin and through occasional descriptions of her clothing and overt disguises. When her physical traits are finally revealed to the reader, they might possibly come as a surprise, especially since her appearance does not fit that of the standard fictional heroine's popular at the time, particularly in that she is described as "tall". The narrative strategy of withholding overt physical description from the reader for such an extended period seems to support, in a very metafictional manner, the Lockean notion of self-in-consciousness by showing the reader that one can know an individual without knowing the details of her external appearance. This example thus emphasizes the immateriality of personal identity, showing that its traits do not necessarily depend upon knowledge of the physical body.

Yet, once again, the implied philosophical comment is complicated through surrounding narrative circumstances; while it is true that the reader does not know what Juliet's physical appearance looks like throughout much of the novel, the characters with which she comes into contact obviously can see her and thus do know that she appears as she is eventually described. Knowing these physical traits helps them to create and perpetuate the Ellis identity in the sense that she is partially interpreted by her physical appearance by those characters who thus act performatively according to their interpretations. Thus, the role of physical appearance in relation to personal identity is left in an ambiguous state. Perhaps, in creating this ambiguity, Burney thus shows the fallacy of relying on the self-in-substance idea since the characters who accept the Ellis identity as true are eventually shown to be grievously wrong, unperceptive fools, a statement that is clarified by the closing circumstances in which those who have most misjudged Juliet according to her appearance, including those who Juliet's uncle designates "the three Furies; Mrs. Howel, Mrs. Ireton, and Mrs. Maple," are banished from the domestic bliss of Harleigh House and are thus understood to be punished through exclusion for their implicit reliance upon the idea of the self-in-substance as they stubbornly interpreted Juliet by her appearance alone (872). But the narrative circumstances also paradoxically show the important and undeniable role that physical appearance plays in the constitution of personal identity in that identity influences appearance by guiding one's choices in presenting themselves to others and that appearance influences identity in the sense that it affects and guides the performative actions of others that help create and perpetuate the personal identity as reality. In relation to the contemporary philosophical notions of the eighteenth-century, then, Burney's novel only insists on exposing the ambiguity inherent in the issues.

While interpretations of The Wanderer as Bildungsroman and those that explore the dynamics of the particular "female difficulties" that are faced by Juliet and the other female characters that are depicted in the narrative are valuable in understanding some facets of the novel, it is clear that Burney's narrative also exists as an important and experimental contribution to the eighteenth-century philosophical and theoretical debates over the nature of personal identity as well as the related issues of performance, performativity, and theatricality. Through innovative and experimental narrative techniques, Burney exposes the ambiguities inherent in these issues, resolutely refusing to present a definitive statement in support of any single interpretation of the ways that personal identity is created and perpetuated on the social stage. Though I have presented what seems central to the debate as depicted in the novel by focusing on analysis of the protagonist's complex circumstances, there are many additional characters and narrative situations presented in the text, as well as in Burney's other novels, that contribute to this particular line of critical scrutiny. Though Barbara Benedict, in her critical work entitled "Identity and Quest: Experimental Experience and the Eighteenth-Century Novel," does not discuss The Wanderer, her observations that "the great theme of the eighteenth-century novel is the wanderer's quest for identity" and that "[novels of this period] expressed the uncertainty of knowing the self—that is, the unknowability of the self in a world of continual change" are provocatively applicable to the study of Burney's work, especially her final novel. In addition to depicting these existential concerns, The Wanderer can clearly be seen to engage philosophical and theoretical issues that were crucial to the eighteenth-century understanding of the self, while both betraying the particular attendant anxieties of the volatile age and employing profoundly innovative narrative techniques that create new dimension of reader involvement with the text. Thus, though it was largely dismissed during the time of its publication, Burney's final novel clearly stands out as a substantially significant piece of intellectual and imaginative literary work, one that offers intriguing insight into eighteenth- and early nineteenth-century notions of the self.

Works Cited

Allen, Emily. "Staging Identity: Frances Burney's Allegory of Genre." Eighteenth-Century Studies. 31.4 (1998): 433-451.

Allison, Henry E. "Locke's Theory of Personal Identity: A Re-Examination." Journal of the History of Ideas. 27.1 (Jan. – March 1966): 41-58.

Anderson, Kathleen. "Frances Burney's The Wanderer: Actress as Virtuous Deceiver." European Romantic Review. 10.4 (Oct. 1999): 424-451.

Austin, Andrea. "Between Women: Frances Burney's The Wanderer." English Studies in Canada. 22.3 (Sept. 1996): 253-266.

Ballaster, Ros. "Narrative Transmigrations: The Oriental Tale and the Novel in Eighteenth-Century Britain." A Companion to the Eighteenth-Century English Novel and Culture. Eds. Paula R. Backscheider and Catherine Ingrassia. Malden, MA: Blackwell Publishing, 2005. 75-96.

Benedict, Barbara. "Identity and Quest: Experimental Experience and the Eighteenth-Century Novel." Eighteenth-Century Novel. 4 (2004): 1-38.

Bial, Henry, ed. The Performance Studies Reader. New York: Routledge, 2004.

Burney, Frances. The Wanderer, or Female Difficulties (1814). Eds. Margaret Anne Doody, Robert L. Mack, and Peter Sabor. Oxford: Oxford University Press, 2001.

Castle, Terry. Masquerade and Civilization: The Carnivalesque in Eighteenth-Century English Culture and Fiction. Stanford: Stanford University Press, 1986.

Carlson, Marvin. Performance: A Critical Introduction. Second Edition. New York: Routledge, 2004.

Cicero. On the Ideal Orator (De Oratore). Trans. James M. May and Jakob Wisse. New York: Oxford University Press, 2001.

Conn, Christopher Hughes. Locke on Essence and Identity. Norwell, MA: Kluwer Academic Publishers, 2003.

Doody, Margaret Anne. "Introduction." The Wanderer, or Female Difficulties (1814). Eds. Margaret Doody, Robert L. Mack, and Peter Sabor. Oxford: Oxford University Press, 2001. vii-xxxvii.

Epstein, Julia. The Iron Pen: Frances Burney and the Politics of Women's Writing. Madison, WI: University of Wisconsin Press, 1989.

Fox, Christopher. "Locke and the Scriblerians: The Discussion of Identity in Early Eighteenth-Century England." Eighteenth-Century Studies. 16.1 (Autumn 1982): 1-25.

Gemmeke, Mascha. Frances Burney and the Female Bildungsroman: An Interpretation of The Wanderer, or Female Difficulties. Frankfurt: Peter Lang, 2003.

Hodgson, Emily. "Staged Insensibility in Burney's Cecilia, Camilla, and The Wanderer: How a Playwright Writes Novels." Eighteenth-Century Fiction. 17.4 (2005): 629-648.

Ingrassia, Catherine. "Introduction." A Companion to the Eighteenth-Century English Novel and Culture. Eds. Paula R. Backscheider and Catherine Ingrassia. Malden, MA: Blackwell Publishing, 2005. 1-21.

Kromm, Jane. "Olivia Furiosa: Maniacal Women from Richardson to Wollstonecraft." Eighteenth-Century Fiction. 16.3 (Spring 2004): 343-372.

Locke, John. An Essay Concerning Human Understanding. Eds. Gary Fuller, Robert Stecker, and John P. Wright. New York: Routledge, 2000.

Manning, Susan. "Sensibility." The Cambridge Companion to English Literature 1740-1830. Eds. Thomas Keymer and Jon Mee. Cambridge: Cambridge University Press, 2004. 80-99.

McCann, Edwin. "Locke on Identity: Matter, Life, and Consciousness." The Empiricists: Critical Essays on Locke, Berkeley, and Hume. Ed. Margaret Atherton. New York: Rowman & Littlefield Publishers, Inc., 1999. 63-88.

McKillop, Alan Dugald. The Early Masters of English Fiction. Lawrence, KS: University Press of Kansas, 1956. 90-91.

Ready, Kathryn J. "Damaris Cudworth Masham, Catharine Trotter Cockburn, and the Feminist Legacy of Locke's Theory of Personal Identity." Eighteenth-Century Studies. 35.4 (2002): 563-576.

Salih, Sara. "'Her Blacks, Her Whites and Her Double Face!': Altering Alterity in The Wanderer." Eighteenth-Century Fiction. 11.3 (April 1999): 301-315.

Scrivener, Michael. "Literature and Politics." The Cambridge Companion to English Literature 1740-1830. Eds. Thomas Keymer and Jon Mee. Cambridge: Cambridge University Press, 2004. 43-60.

Spacks, Patricia Meyer. "Privacy, Dissimulation and Propriety: Frances Burney and Jane Austen." Eighteenth-Century Fiction. 12.4 (Summer 2000): 515-531.

Spoel, Philippa M. "Rereading the Elocutionists: The Rhetoric of Thomas Sheridan's A Course on Elocution and John Walker's Elements of Elocution." Rhetorica. 19.1 (Winter 2001): 49-91.

Straub, Kristina. Divided Fictions: Fanny Burney and Feminine Strategy. Lexington, KY: University Press of Kentucky, 1987.

"tabula rasa, n." The Oxford English Dictionary. 2nd ed. 1989. OED Online. Oxford University Press. University of Kansas Libraries, Lawrence, KS. 9 April 2007. <http://dictionary.oed.com.www2.lib.ku.edu:2048/cgi/entry/50245914>.

Thiel, Udo. "Self-Consciousness and Personal Identity." The Cambridge History of Eighteenth-Century Philosophy. Vol. 1. Ed. Knud Haakonssen. Cambridge: Cambridge University Press, 2006. 286-318.

Walker, William. Locke, Literary Criticism, and Philosophy. Cambride: Cambridge University Press, 1994.

www.ingramcontent.com/pod-product-compliance
Lightning Source LLC
Chambersburg PA
CBHW071414290426
44108CB00014B/1819